116TH

HARLEM

UPPER WEST SIDE

Hudson River

Central Park

59TH

UPPER EAST SIDE

42ND

34TH

FIFTH AVE

23RD

MIDTOWN

14TH

Chelsea

8TH

Flatiron

Greenwich Village

Gramercy Park

HOUSTON ST

East Village

SoHo

CANAL ST

Little Italy

LOWER MANHATTAN

Chinatown

East River

N

PAULA KELLY

TIMELESS

NEW YORK

TIMELESS

NEW YORK

A Literary

and

Photographic

Tribute

PAUL COUGHLIN

UNIVERSE

Dedication

For Carol Carson, Dick Jenney, Jane Perkel, Robert Perkel, Connie Poster, Sabina Roseman, and Jerry Sheehan.

Acknowledgments

A heartfelt thank you to Donald Williams—one of the nicest things about the Big Apple; to Martha Kaplan for her support; to Sandy Gilbert for her inexhaustible energy; and to Kerry Acker for providing eloquence.

Grateful acknowledgment is made to the people who helped in the making of this book; among them, Robert and Jane Gordon, Aura Donaldson, Shalom Ben-Yosef, Susan Golomb, E. B. Beck, Mary Osborne, Karl Wilder, Frank Marsciano, Stacy Shub, Joyce Denebrink, Judy Kern, Jane Kronick, Joyce Phillip, Mary Hazel, and Patsy Zindel. For their photographic assistance I thank Josh Weiss, David Rajuan, Zeke Martin, Ed Lynch, Troy Hazen, Ria Demeo, Ben Fernando, Ed Dougherty, Rick Lopez, Elliot Spector, and the Flash Team: Joe, Sam, Khaled, and Brahim. A thank you also goes to fellow photographers Marti Andersen, Hector Alers, and Joan R. Meisel; and the Cortland Jessup Gallery. Thank you to Jill Dunbar and Jenny Feder of Three Lives and Co. for your support and encouragement. A very special thank you goes to Harry J. Abrahamsen, Sr., and Carol A. Bass.

First published in the United States of America in 1998

by UNIVERSE PUBLISHING

A division of Rizzoli International Publications, Inc.

300 Park Avenue South

New York, NY 10010

00 01 02/10 9 8 7 6 5 4 3 2

Library of Congress Catalog Card Number: 98-61126

Printed in Singapore

Endpapers

Front: *Prometheus* by Paul Manship (Rockefeller Center); viewer (Battery Park)
Back: *Charging Bull* by Arturo DiModica (Bowling Green); '21' Club (21 West 52nd Street)

Page 7: subway sign (42nd Street and eighth Avenue)

Design and typography by Carol Devine Carson and Abby Weintraub

Contents

A city like this one makes me dream tall and feel in on things.

—Toni Morrison

NEW YORK IS THE PLACE WHERE I FEEL MOST PASSIONATE—IT IS BOTH MY MUSE AND THE MAJOR SUBJECT OF MY PHOTOGRAPHS. UNDER NEW YORK'S SPELL, I HAVE BECOME AN INTREPID PHOTOGRAPHER, WALKING THROUGH BLIZZARDS AND HEAT WAVES, CLIMBING ACROSS ROOFTOPS, SKIRTING PAST SECURITY GUARDS—IN THE ATTEMPT TO PHOTOGRAPH THE CITY IN ALL ITS DAILY IMPROVISATIONAL BEAUTY.

THE RESULT OF THIS NEARLY IMPOSSIBLE ENDEAVOR IS *TIMELESS NEW YORK*. HERE IS A NEW YORK FOR THE CAREFUL OBSERVER—THE PLAY OF LIGHT THAT TRANSFORMS ORDINARY DAYS INTO ROMANTIC SCENES, THE SUBTLE SEASONAL CHANGES THAT CAST DRAMATIC SHADOWS IN UNLIKELY PLACES, THE MÉLANGE OF TEXTURES, AND, MOST OF ALL, THE IMPROBABLE DIVERSITY. OTHER CITIES HAVE SKYSCRAPERS, BUT NEW YORK HAS CAST-IRON PALACES, TENEMENTS, TOWNHOUSES, AND ART DECO TOWERS ALL CRAMMED TOGETHER, GIVING US A CITY WITH A TRULY DEMOCRATIC CHARACTER.

CITY PLANNERS MAY TRY TO SHAPE IT, BUT THE TRUE COLOR OF THE CITY COMES FROM NEW YORKERS THEMSELVES. THE CITY IS A JUXTAPOSITION OF THE OLD, NEW, AND UNEXPECTED. TURNING A CORNER, YOU ARE LIKELY TO EXPERIENCE SOMETHING COMPLETELY DIFFERENT FROM THE CORNER BEFORE. I ONCE SAW A WOMAN WALKING A REINDEER DOWN 51ST STREET. THERE WERE MANY PEOPLE AROUND, BUT NO ONE BATTED AN EYELASH. THINGS HAPPEN IN NEW YORK THAT NO ONE COULD ORCHESTRATE— THEY JUST HAPPEN.

MUCH HAS BEEN WRITTEN ABOUT THIS CITY OF FLEETING ENCOUNTERS, IMAGES, AND FRAGMENTS. I HAVE CHOSEN THE LUMINOUS WORDS OF SUCH WRITERS AS E. B. WHITE, WALT WHITMAN, HART CRANE, EDITH WHARTON, AND ANAÏS NIN TO ACCOMPANY MY PHOTOGRAPHS AS THEY OFFER FURTHER INSIGHTS INTO THE SINGULAR MAGIC AND RICHNESS OF NEW YORK.

—PAUL COUGHLIN

Then the New York I miss. The city of imagination that is a skyscape of towers and deep shadows and sharp lights, a little medieval. This once allowed you to love the city forever . . . —Grace Paley

THE TWISTED STREETS OF LOWER MANHATTAN WERE ORIGINALLY LAID OUT BY THE DUTCH. MANY OF THE STREET NAMES STILL REFLECT THESE ORIGINS: BEAVER STREET WAS THE EARLY CENTER OF THE FUR TRADE, PEARL STREET WAS LITERALLY PAVED WITH OYSTER SHELLS, AND WALL STREET WAS NAMED AFTER AN ACTUAL WALL USED FOR FORTIFICATION OF THE CITY. AS THE CITY GREW, RESIDENTIAL SECTIONS WERE ESTABLISHED FURTHER UP THE ISLAND; FEW PEOPLE LIVE IN LOWER MANHATTAN, AS THE AREA IS ALMOST EXCLUSIVELY USED TO HOUSE SUCH INSTITUTIONS AS OFFICES OF COMMERCE, GOVERNMENT, AND INTERNATIONAL BANKING.

AMONG THE EARLY DOWNTOWN SKYSCRAPERS THAT GAVE THE NEW YORK SKYLINE ITS ROMANTIC CHARACTER IS THE WOOLWORTH BUILDING. DESIGNED BY CASS GILBERT, THIS STRUCTURE WAS THE WORLD'S TALLEST BUILDING FROM 1913 TO 1930. AMONG THE WHIMSICAL TOUCHES IN THE LOBBY IS THE GOTHIC-INSPIRED GROTESQUE OF FRANK WOOLWORTH COUNTING HIS NICKELS AND DIMES. THE BUILDING COST 13.5 MILLION DOLLARS TO BUILD AND WAS PAID FOR ENTIRELY IN CASH.

SOUTH STREET SEAPORT

(FULTON, FRONT, AND SOUTH STREETS)

Walking alone up South Street Behind the wharfhouses, ships raise shadowy skeletons against the night. —John Dos Passos

KNOWN AS "THE STREET OF SHIPS," SOUTH STREET WAS THE CITY'S MOST IMPORTANT SHIPPING CENTER DURING THE NINETEENTH CENTURY. TODAY THE SEAPORT IS AN OPEN-AIR MUSEUM COMPRISED OF HISTORIC BUILDINGS AND SHIPS, SHOPS, AND GALLERIES. SCHERMERHORN ROW, A GROUP OF GEORGIAN-FEDERAL–STYLE STRUCTURES THAT WERE BUILT IN 1811–12 TO HOUSE SHIP CHANDLERS, IS NOW A CENTRAL COMPONENT OF THE PORT.

DOCKED AT THE PIER IS AN IMPORTANT COLLECTION OF HISTORIC SAILING VESSELS INCLUDING THE *ANDREW FLETCHER*, A NINETEENTH-CENTURY PADDLE WHEELER; THE *AMBROSE LIGHT-SHIP* (1907); THE FOUR-MASTED 321-FOOT *PEKING* (1911); THE THREE-MASTED *WAVERTREE* (1885); AND THE *PIONEER* SCHOONER (1885), WHERE ON BOARD PARTICIPANTS ARE INVITED TO HOIST THE SAILS AND SAIL THE SHIP.

Gorgeous clouds of the sunset! drench

with your splendor me, or the men and

women generations after me! . . .

Stand up tall masts of Mannahatta!

stand up, beautiful hills of Brooklyn!

—Walt Whitman

BROOKLYN BRIDGE

(LINKING MANHATTAN [CITY HALL PARK]
AND BROOKLYN [CADMAN PLAZA]
OVER THE EAST RIVER)

ONE OF THE WONDERS OF THE NINETEENTH CENTURY, THE BROOKLYN BRIDGE, OPENED IN 1883, WAS THEN THE LARGEST BRIDGE IN THE WORLD AS WELL AS THE FIRST STEEL-CABLE SUSPENSION BRIDGE.

DESIGNER JOHN A. ROEBLING DIED BEFORE THE BRIDGE WAS COMPLETED. CONSTRUCTION WAS CONTINUED UNDER THE DIRECTION OF HIS THIRTY-TWO-YEAR-OLD SON, WASHINGTON, WHO IN TURN BECAME SEVERELY ILL AND DIRECTED THE ENTIRE OPERATION FROM HIS BEDROOM WINDOW WITH THE AID OF A TELESCOPE.

THE BEAUTY OF THE BRIDGE HAS INSPIRED SUCH POETS AS WALT WHITMAN, HART CRANE, AND ELIZABETH BISHOP, AS WELL AS PAINTER JOSEPH STELLA. A STROLL ACROSS THE PEDESTRIAN BOARDWALK ON THE BRIDGE IS ONE OF THE MOST EXHILARATING EXPERIENCES NEW YORK HAS TO OFFER.

NEW YORK STOCK EXCHANGE

IN 1792 A GROUP OF TWENTY-FOUR BROKERS MET UNDER THE SHADE OF A BUTTONWOOD TREE ON WALL STREET, AND FROM THIS BEGINNING THE LARGEST SECURITIES EXCHANGE IN THE WORLD WAS BORN.

THE PRESENT NEO-RENAISSANCE–STYLE BUILDING, DESIGNED BY GEORGE B. POST IN 1903, HAS A TRIANGULAR PEDIMENT REPRESENTING "INTEGRITY PROTECTING THE WORKS OF MAN." WHEN IT WAS DISCOVERED THAT THIS SCULPTURAL ENSEMBLE HAD GREATLY DETERIORATED, THE ORIGINAL STONE MYTHOLOGICAL FIGURES WERE REPLACED WITH METAL ONES (1936). THIS WAS DONE SECRETLY SO THAT THE PUBLIC WOULD NOT KNOW THAT THE STOCK EXCHANGE WAS VULNERABLE.

THE TRADING FLOOR, ONE OF NEW YORK'S GRAND SPACES, IS TWO-THIRDS THE SIZE OF A FOOTBALL FIELD. FIFTY MILLION SHARES OF STOCK ARE TRADED DAILY.

FEDERAL HALL

(28 WALL STREET, CORNER OF NASSAU STREET)

FEDERAL HALL, NOW A NATIONAL MONUMENT, IS THE SITE WHERE GEORGE WASHINGTON WAS INAUGURATED INTO OFFICE AS THE FIRST U.S. PRESIDENT. THE CURRENT STRUCTURE WAS BUILT IN 1842 (TOWN & DAVIS). THE ORIGINAL FEDERAL HALL WAS DEMOLISHED IN 1812 AND SOLD FOR SCRAP FOR 425 DOLLARS.

TRINITY CHURCH AND CHURCHYARD

(BROADWAY AT WALL STREET)

IN THE MIDST OF SKYSCRAPERS SITS TRINITY CHURCH, WITH THE OLDEST CONGREGATION IN NEW YORK, FOUNDED IN 1697. RICHARD UPJOHN, WHO DESIGNED THE PRESENT ENGLISH-GOTHIC CHURCH OF 1846, WAS INNOVATIVE IN HIS USE OF BROWNSTONE, A SANDSTONE MATERIAL CONSIDERED TOO COMMON FOR SUCH AN IMPORTANT STRUCTURE.

THE MAGNIFICENT SCULPTURED BRONZE DOORS WERE DESIGNED BY RICHARD MORRIS HUNT AS A MEMORIAL TO FINANCIER JOHN JACOB ASTOR. THE CHURCHYARD IS A WELCOME BIT OF GREENERY, AND ON COLD WINTER DAYS BUSINESSMEN AND -WOMEN HAVE EVEN BEEN SEEN EATING SANDWICHES IN THE PEWS.

WORLD TRADE CENTER
(TWIN TOWERS)
(CHURCH STREET, BETWEEN
LIBERTY AND VESEY STREETS)

THESE MONOLITHIC TOWERS WERE COMPLETED IN 1977 (MINORU YAMASAKI & ASSOC.) AT AN ESTIMATED COST OF 700 MILLION DOLLARS. THEY ARE HOME TO MORE THAN FIVE HUNDRED INTERNATIONAL CORPORATIONS THAT PROVIDE EMPLOYMENT FOR FIFTY THOUSAND PEOPLE. THE TOWERS HAVE OBSERVATION DECKS, A BAR, AND RESTAURANTS—INCLUDING THE PENTHOUSE WINDOWS ON THE WORLD. THE BUILDINGS TOOK OVER TWELVE YEARS TO COMPLETE, STAND 1,350 FEET HIGH, AND HAVE 110 FLOORS. IN 1974 FRENCH ACROBAT PHILIPPE PETIT PERFORMED A TIGHTROPE WALK BETWEEN THE TOPS OF THE TWO TOWERS. AND IN 1975 MOUNTAIN CLIMBER GEORGE WILLIG SCALED TO THE TOP.

STATUE OF LIBERTY

(LIBERTY ISLAND [BEDLOE'S ISLAND],

NEW YORK HARBOR)

FOR MILLIONS OF PEOPLE WHO IMMIGRATED TO THE UNITED STATES FOR A BETTER LIFE, THE STATUE OF LIBERTY WAS THEIR FIRST VISION OF AMERICA. "LIBERTY ENLIGHTENING THE WORLD" (THE STATUE'S OFFICIAL NAME) WAS A GIFT FROM THE FRENCH PEOPLE COMMEMORATING A SHARED EXPRESSION OF FREEDOM. CREATED BY ALSATIAN SCULPTOR FRÉDÉRIC-AUGUSTE BARTHOLDI, AND ENGINEERED BY GUSTAV EIFFEL (OF EIFFEL TOWER FAME), THE 22-STORY, 225-TON MONUMENT WAS UNVEILED WHEN A TRICOLORED FLAG WAS LIFTED OFF HER FACE ON OCTOBER 28, 1886. HER SHEER MAGNITUDE IS IMPRESSIVE: SHE STANDS 151 FEET TALL, AND HAS A 3-FOOT MOUTH AND A 35-FOOT WAIST. HOWEVER, THE GREEN COPPER GOWN SHE WEARS IS ONLY ONE-TENTH OF AN INCH THICK, RIVETED TO A STEEL FRAME. ON HER HEAD IS A SEVEN-POINTED CROWN, SYMBOLIZING THE SPIRIT OF LIBERTY THAT RADIATES FROM HER TO ALL SEVEN CONTINENTS.

DOWNTOWN NEIGHBORHOODS

People from villages and small towns, people accustomed to the . . . friendliness of neighborhood over the fence living, are unaware . . . the city is literally a composite of tens of thousands of tiny neighborhood units . . . . —E. B. White

THE SOUL OF NEW YORK CITY CAN BE FOUND IN ITS HUNDREDS OF HIGHLY INDIVIDUALIZED NEIGHBORHOODS. A GLANCE DOWN A TREE-LINED SIDE STREET IN SUCH RESIDENTIAL ENCLAVES AS CHINATOWN, THE LOWER EAST SIDE, AND GREENWICH VILLAGE WILL REVEAL A DISTINCT MICROCOSM OF LIFE.

A WALK THROUGH ONE OF THESE DOWNTOWN NEIGHBORHOODS COULD TAKE YOU, IN QUICK SUCCESSION, THROUGH CONCENTRATED MINIATURE VERSIONS OF CHINA, INDIA, ITALY, AND RUSSIA. MORE THAN EIGHTY LANGUAGES ARE SPOKEN, AND RESTAURANTS SERVE EVERY TYPE OF FOOD IMAGINABLE. TO LIVE IN NEW YORK IS TO LIVE IN THE WORLD.

CHINATOWN

(NEIGHBORHOOD AROUND MOTT STREET, SOUTH OF CANAL STREET ON THE EAST SIDE)

IN THE 1850S, CHINESE IMMIGRANTS WENT TO THE WEST COAST TO MINE IN CALIFORNIA'S GOLD FIELDS. DISAPPOINTED, MANY CAME TO NEW YORK WITH THE HOPE OF MAKING ENOUGH MONEY TO RETURN TO CHINA, AND THEY ESTABLISHED CHINATOWN.

TODAY THERE ARE TWO DIFFERENT CHINATOWNS— ONE FOR THE TOURIST, AND THE OTHER, A SELF-CONTAINED NEIGHBORHOOD OF PEOPLE (MANY WHO HAVE LIVED HERE FOR GENERATIONS). CHINESE RESTAURANTS ABOUND, AND MERCHANTS SELLING EXOTIC VEGETABLES, LIVE TURTLES, AND WIND-DRIED DUCK FROM STALLS CROWD THE SIDEWALKS. SO INSULATED IS THIS AREA FROM THE REST OF NEW YORK THAT WE HEAR TALES OF NINETY-YEAR-OLD WOMEN BORN HERE WHO NEVER LEARNED TO SPEAK ENGLISH, AND NEVER ONCE STEPPED OUT OF CHINATOWN.

CHINESE HERITAGE IS EVIDENT DURING CHINESE NEW YEAR (THE FIRST FULL MOON AFTER THE NINETEENTH OF JANUARY), WHEN REVELERS AND AN ENORMOUS DRAGON DANCE DOWN THE TWISTED STREETS CHASING AWAY EVIL SPIRITS.

Little Italy

This residential area became home to thousands of Italians who immigrated into New York at the turn of the century. Today the narrow streets are lined with scores of Italian restaurants, grocery stores, and bakeries, many of which date back to the 1880s. Occasionally you see laundry flapping from a window or a pot of basil growing on a fire escape—small reminders to a people of their homes back in Naples.

The Feast of Saint Gennaro (the patron saint of Naples) is celebrated along Mulberry Street every September. Streets are arched with lights, Neapolitan bands play, and a life-sized statue is paraded down Mulberry while the devoted pin money to his image.

LOWER EAST SIDE

(BETWEEN HOUSTON AND GRAND STREETS,

AND THE BOWERY)

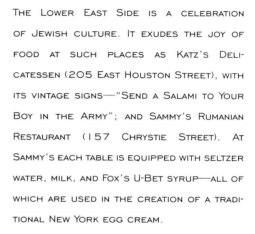

THE LOWER EAST SIDE IS A CELEBRATION OF JEWISH CULTURE. IT EXUDES THE JOY OF FOOD AT SUCH PLACES AS KATZ'S DELICATESSEN (205 EAST HOUSTON STREET), WITH ITS VINTAGE SIGNS—"SEND A SALAMI TO YOUR BOY IN THE ARMY"; AND SAMMY'S RUMANIAN RESTAURANT (157 CHRYSTIE STREET). AT SAMMY'S EACH TABLE IS EQUIPPED WITH SELTZER WATER, MILK, AND FOX'S U-BET SYRUP—ALL OF WHICH ARE USED IN THE CREATION OF A TRADITIONAL NEW YORK EGG CREAM.

IN 1929 A LAW WAS PASSED THAT REQUIRED ALL TENEMENTS TO HAVE AN INDOOR TOILET AND A WINDOW. THE OWNER OF 97 ORCHARD STREET DECIDED INSTEAD TO SAVE MONEY AND RENT OUT ONLY THE GROUND-FLOOR RETAIL SPACE, LEAVING THE APARTMENTS ABOVE VACANT. YEARS LATER IT WAS DISCOVERED THAT THE "FLATS," AS THESE UPPER APARTMENTS WERE CALLED, WERE SO PERFECTLY PRESERVED THAT TODAY 97 ORCHARD STREET IS THE HOME OF THE LOWER EAST SIDE TENEMENT MUSEUM.

SoHo

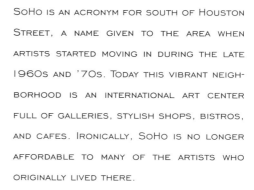

SoHo is an acronym for south of Houston Street, a name given to the area when artists started moving in during the late 1960s and '70s. Today this vibrant neighborhood is an international art center full of galleries, stylish shops, bistros, and cafes. Ironically, SoHo is no longer affordable to many of the artists who originally lived there.

SoHo has the heaviest concentration of cast-iron buildings in the world. These prefabricated edifices, built between 1856 and 1895, encompass almost every major classic architectural style imaginable. The Haughwout building at 488 Broadway (pictured to the right) is a cast-iron masterpiece modeled after Venice's Sansovino Library.

GREENWICH VILLAGE

GREENWICH VILLAGE HAS ALWAYS HAD ITS NON-CONFORMISTS. AS EARLY AS 1811, WHEN THE CITY'S STREETS WERE ALIGNED TO CREATE THE GRID SYSTEM, THE PEOPLE OF GREENWICH VILLAGE PROTESTED, AND CITY OFFICIALS WERE SYMPATHETIC. THE VILLAGE HAS BEEN IDIOSYN-CRATIC EVER SINCE—WEST 4TH STREET INTER-SECTS WEST 10TH STREET, AND AT ONE POINT WAVERLY PLACE DIVIDES AND INTERSECTS ITSELF. WRITER LAWRENCE BLOCK NOTES, "YOU CANNOT BUT REALIZE THAT YOU HAVE STEPPED INTO A NON-EUCLIDEAN UNIVERSE, THE GREAT SECURITY OF LIVING IN AN OR-DERED WORLD WHERE PARALLEL LINES NEVER MEET IS LOST FOREVER TO YOU NOW."

DESPITE A GREAT DEAL OF CHANGE AND RE-BUILDING, THE AREA STILL HAS THE INTIMATE SCALE THAT ATTRACTED SUCH PEOPLE AS MARK TWAIN, O. HENRY, AND EDNA ST. VINCENT MILLAY TO LIVE HERE.

Washington
Memorial Arch

(Washington Square North at Fifth Avenue)

The Washington Memorial Arch marks the beginning of Fifth Avenue. Created by Stanford White (McKim, Mead & White), this marble arch honors George Washington and replaced a temporary wood and stucco arch constructed in 1889 to commemorate the inauguration of the first president. The temporary monument was so well received that the current arch was constructed in 1892.

In 1917, artist Marcel Duchamp and five other Village residents climbed the 110 steps to the top of the arch and declared Greenwich Village an independent country.

During the 1940s, a homeless man was able to live undetected inside the arch for a few months. He was discovered only when he hung out his laundry from the top. In the 1970s Bulgarian artist Christo covered the entire arch with netting, turning Stanford White's nineteenth-century monument into twentieth-century modern art.

Brownstone houses . . . in orderly procession, like a young ladies' boarding school taking its daily exercise. . . . All so much alike that one could understand how easy it would be for a dinner guest to go to the wrong house. . . . —Edith Wharton

THE ROW

(WASHINGTON SQUARE NORTH BETWEEN FIFTH AVENUE AND UNIVERSITY PLACE)

BUILT BETWEEN 1832 AND 1839, THESE ARISTOCRATIC HOUSES ARE BELIEVED TO BE THE FINEST EXAMPLES OF GREEK REVIVAL ARCHITECTURE IN THE UNITED STATES. THIS WAS THE SETTING FOR HENRY JAMES'S *WASHINGTON SQUARE*. "THIS PORTION OF NEW YORK," JAMES WROTE, "APPEARS TO MANY PERSONS THE MOST DELECTABLE. IT HAS A KIND OF ESTABLISHED REPOSE WHICH IS NOT OF FREQUENT OCCURRENCE IN OTHER QUARTERS OF THE LONG SHRILL CITY."

AMONG THE LITERARY AND ARTISTIC CIRCLE OF NEW YORKERS WHO LIVED ON "THE ROW" ARE EDITH WHARTON, JOHN DOS PASSOS, AND EDWARD HOPPER.

East Village

The East Village, a group of diverse neighborhoods bonded together by their proximity, is now populated by club-goers and tattooed and pierced types who wander around like characters from a Hieronymus Bosch painting. There are ethnic enclaves of Greeks, Poles, Puerto Ricans, Russians, and Ukrainians, as well as a large artistic community.

During the mid-nineteenth century, the area along Astor Place and Lafayette Street was the most fashionable address in New York. Remaining from this period is a crumbling façade of a group of buildings called Colonnade Row (built 1831–33) at 428–434 Lafayette Street.

The great iron and glass subway kiosk at Astor Place was designed by Heins & La Farge in 1904—the same men who designed the Cathedral of Saint John The Divine.

GRAMERCY PARK

(20TH TO 21ST STREETS BETWEEN
PARK AND THIRD AVENUES)

THIS ELEGANT PARK OF 1831 WAS CREATED BY
SAMUEL B. RUGGLES WHEN HE PURCHASED
A PARCEL OF LAND WITH THE INTENTION
OF BUILDING A RESIDENTIAL NEIGHBORHOOD
AROUND A SMALL ENGLISH-STYLE PARK. LOT
OWNERS WOULD BE GIVEN THE PRIVILEGE OF
HAVING A KEY TO THE PARK—A PRACTICE THAT
CONTINUES TO THIS DAY.

SURROUNDING THE PARK ARE SOME CHARMING
GREEK REVIVAL BROWNSTONES OF 1846 SUCH
AS NUMBERS 3 AND 4 GRAMERCY PARK WEST,
WITH THEIR SHARED CAST-IRON PORCH AND
CLIMBING WISTERIA. THE TWO LAMPS WITH FIVE-
POINTED TOPS SIGNIFY THAT THIS ONCE WAS THE
HOME OF A MAYOR, A TRADITION DATING BACK TO
THE DUTCH—THE LAMPS WERE LIT ONLY WHEN
THE MAYOR WAS HOME. THE PLAYERS CLUB
(16 GRAMERCY PARK SOUTH), THE FORMER
RESIDENCE OF EDWIN BOOTH, IS NOW A PRESTI-
GIOUS PRIVATE CLUB FOR THEATER PROFESSION-
ALS. NEXT DOOR IS THE NATIONAL ARTS CLUB.
FOUNDED IN 1884, IT IS A POPULAR PLACE FOR
EXHIBITIONS, BOOK SIGNINGS, AND READINGS.

Chelsea

*The Chelsea was not part of America,
had no vacuum cleaners, no rules, no taste,
no shame . . . it was a ceaseless party.*
— *Arthur Miller*

This tree-lined neighborhood is an eclectic mix of handsome townhouses, gentrified tenements, and architectural surprises such as the Empire Diner (210 Tenth Avenue). Built in 1943 with its art deco styling of black glass and stainless steel, the Empire is the classic American diner.

Chelsea's great landmark is the Chelsea Hotel, at 222 West 23rd Street. Erected in 1884 in the Victorian gothic style, the Chelsea became the haunt of artists, writers, and entertainers, including Sarah Bernhardt, Arthur Miller, and Tennessee Williams. Sunflowers, the symbol of the aesthetic movement, are cast in the Chelsea's iron balconies. The lobby— the most eccentric in all New York— resembles an avant-garde vision of a Bloomsbury salon. It was at the Hotel that the Welsh poet Dylan Thomas spent his last days, where Andy Warhol shot his underground film *Chelsea Girls*, and Nancy Spungen, the girlfriend of Sid Vicious (of Sex Pistols fame), met her demise.

I found myself agape, admiring a sky-scraper, the prow of the Flatiron Building to be particular, ploughing up through the traffic of Broadway and Fifth in the late afternoon light. —H. G. Wells

FLATIRON DISTRICT

(FIFTH AVENUE SOUTH OF 23RD STREET)

RESEMBLING A TRIANGULAR PALAZZO SOARING ABOVE BROADWAY, THE RENAISSANCE-STYLE FLATIRON BUILDING HAS FASCINATED NEW YORKERS SINCE ITS CONSTRUCTION IN 1902 (D. H. BURHAM & CO.). THE 21-STORY, 285-FOOT FREESTANDING STRUCTURE SEEMED TO DEFY GRAVITY. PHOTOGRAPHER ALFRED STIEGLITZ WROTE THAT IT "APPEARED TO BE MOVING . . . LIKE THE BOW OF A MONSTER OCEAN STEAMER— A PICTURE OF AMERICA STILL IN THE MAKING."

THE SURROUNDING AREA, KNOWN AS THE FLATIRON DISTRICT, IS ALIVE WITH THE ACTIVITY OF MODELS, PHOTOGRAPHERS, AND STYLISTS, FOR A GREAT PERCENTAGE OF COMMERCIAL PHOTOGRAPHY STUDIOS ARE BASED HERE.

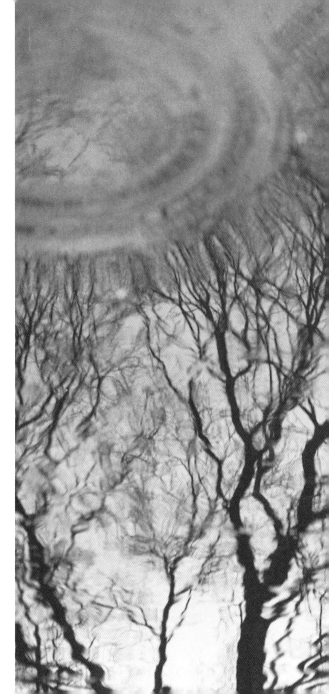

There is no question there is an unseen world, the question is, how far is it from midtown, and how late is it open? —Woody Allen

THIS IS THE HEART OF NEW YORK, SWELLING WITH ACTIVITY, NOISE, AND EXHILARATION. WHEN PEOPLE VISUALIZE MANHATTAN, THEY PICTURE MIDTOWN'S MAJOR SKYSCRAPERS, THE THEATER DISTRICT, AND SUCH PREEMINENT LANDMARKS AS ROCKEFELLER CENTER AND THE UNITED NATIONS. (THE U.N., LOCATED AT FIRST AVENUE AND 42ND AND 48TH STREETS, AND BUILT ON EIGHTEEN ACRES, LEGALLY ISN'T PART OF NEW YORK—IT HAS ITS OWN POST OFFICE AND SECURITY FORCE.)

GRAND CENTRAL TERMINAL (42ND STREET BETWEEN VANDERBILT AND LEXINGTON AVENUES), IS A MASTERPIECE OF ARCHITECTURAL DESIGN (REED & STERN AND WARREN & WETMORE). FINISHED IN 1913, ITS MAIN CONCOURSE HAS A PAINTED CEILING BY WHITNEY WARREN (WITH PAUL HELLEU AND CHARLES BASING) REPRESENTING THE CONSTELLATIONS FROM THE VIEWPOINT OF GOD, COMPLETE WITH ILLUMINATED STARS. THE STATION EPITOMIZES A TIME WHEN THE ROMANCE OF TRAIN TRAVEL WAS IN FULL BLOOM.

Skyscrapers . . . like extravagant pins
in a cushion . . . with flash of innumer-
able windows and flicker of subordinate
gilt . . . —Henry James

EMPIRE STATE BUILDING

(FIFTH AVENUE AND 34TH STREET)

THE EMPIRE STATE BUILDING IS THE QUINTES-
SENTIAL NEW YORK SKYSCRAPER. BUILT IN 1931
(SHREVE, LAMB & HARMON), DURING THE GREAT
DEPRESSION, THE BUILDING WAS CONSTRUCTED
IN THE ART DECO STYLE, PARTICULARLY SEEN IN ITS
LOBBY'S GEOMETRIC PATTERNS OF GLASS, MARBLE,
AND STAINLESS STEEL.

CONSTRUCTED OF INDIANA LIMESTONE AND
TRIMMED WITH STEEL AND GRANITE, THE BUILD-
ING STANDS MORE THAN A QUARTER OF A MILE
HIGH, AT 1,454 FEET. AT NIGHT ITS STEEL
SPIRE IS ILLUMINATED WITH COLOR COMBINA-
TIONS THAT SIGNIFY SPECIAL EVENTS AND
HOLIDAYS. THE OBSERVATION DECK OFFERS A
BREATHTAKING VIEW OF THE CITY.

HERALD SQUARE

(34TH STREET FROM BROADWAY TO

SEVENTH AVENUE)

MACY'S DEPARTMENT STORE DOMINATES THE SQUARE WITH ITS TWO MILLION SQUARE FEET OF FLOOR SPACE—IT IS SAID TO BE THE LARGEST STORE ON EARTH. IN 1924, PUPPETEER TONY SARG DESIGNED THE FIRST INFLATABLE CHARACTER BALLOON, WHICH INAUGURATED THE MACY'S THANKSGIVING DAY PARADE.

THE GREAT BRONZE CLOCK STANDING IN HERALD SQUARE, WITH ITS BELL RINGERS STRIKING THE HOUR, WAS ORIGINALLY ON TOP OF THE NEW YORK HERALD BUILDING. WHEN THE BUILDING, WHICH STOOD NORTH OF THE SQUARE, WAS DEMOLISHED IN 1921, THE VENETIAN-STYLE CLOCK WAS MOVED TO ITS PRESENT SITE.

The Museum of Modern Art
(MoMA)
(11 West 53rd Street)

The world's foremost museum of modern masters, founded in 1929, showcases a comprehensive collection of international works of art, including Picasso, van Gogh, and Warhol, as well as film and industrial design. The international-style building (completed in 1939) was designed by Edward Durrell Stone and Philip Goodwin, with later additions by Philip Johnson Architects and Cesar Pelli & Associates. MoMA's garden, a tranquil sanctuary in the heart of midtown, offers a popular concert program.

New York Public Library
(Fifth Avenue between 40th and 42nd streets)

This distinctive structure (Carrère and Hastings, 1898–1911) is beaux arts style at its best. The famous stone lions, sculpted by Edward Clark Potter, guard a collection of over thirty-six million books, manuscripts, art, and ephemera in three thousand languages and dialects. The fifth-floor reading rooms cover two city blocks and can accommodate five thousand people. Among the collection can be found Thomas Jefferson's handwritten draft of the Declaration of Independence, a stuffed bear that inspired A. A. Milne to write *Winnie the Pooh,* and George Washington's farewell speech to the nation, penned in his own hand. But the real beauty of the Library is that it is public, so everyone has access to its wealth of rare books and documents.

Proud towers that augmented ecclesiology with jaunty modernity by sporting hubcaps and hood ornaments in place of griffins and saints—hence the Chrysler Building.

—Robert A. M. Stern

CHRYSLER BUILDING

(405 LEXINGTON AVENUE AT 42ND STREET)

A MODERNIST'S MASTERPIECE OF ARCHITECTURE (WILLIAM VAN ALEN)—PERHAPS THE MOST IMAGINATIVE SKYSCRAPER IN THE U.S. ITS FANCIFUL SPIRE WAS SECRETLY CONSTRUCTED IN THE BUILDING'S INTERIOR, THEN HOISTED INTO PLACE AND BOLTED DOWN IN NINETY MINUTES—MAKING THE CHRYSLER BUILDING (1930) THE FIRST STRUCTURE TO SURPASS THE EIFFEL TOWER IN HEIGHT.

THE STAINLESS STEEL TOWER, 1,048 FEET HIGH, HAS A WHIMSICAL DISPLAY OF HUBCAPS WITH WINGS, RADIATOR-CAP GARGOYLES, AND A BAND OF ABSTRACT AUTOMOBILES. THE LOBBY IS LINED WITH RED-VEINED AFRICAN MARBLE, AND THE ELEVATOR CARS, WITH THEIR INLAID EXOTIC WOODS, ARE AMONG THE MOST INVENTIVE ANYWHERE.

ROCKEFELLER CENTER

(FIFTH TO SIXTH AVENUES, BETWEEN
WEST 48TH AND 51ST STREETS)

ROCKEFELLER CENTER IS A MODERNIST'S VISION OF ART, ARCHITECTURE, ENTERTAINMENT, AND COMMERCE. DEVELOPED BY JOHN D. ROCKEFELLER, JR., IN THE 1930S, THE COMPLEX IS AN OUTSTANDING EXAMPLE OF ART DECO STYLE. ITS PUBLIC SPACES PARADE WORKS OF ART WITH MYTHOLOGICAL THEMES, SUCH AS THE GILDED BRONZE *PROMETHEUS* BY PAUL MANSHIP LORDING OVER THE ICE RINK (WHICH DOUBLES AS AN OUTDOOR RESTAURANT IN WARMER MONTHS), AND THE BRONZE *ATLAS*, BY LEE LAURIE, WHICH FACES SAINT PATRICK'S CATHEDRAL ON FIFTH AVENUE.

RADIO CITY MUSIC HALL, THE QUINTESSENTIAL ART DECO MOVIE PALACE, IS PART OF THE ORIGNAL COMPLEX. ON THE SIXTY-FIFTH FLOOR OF THE CENTER IS THE RAINBOW ROOM, WHICH RETAINS THE ATMOSPHERE AND MAGIC OF A 1930S SUPPER CLUB.

Plaza Hotel

(Fifth Avenue and Central Park South)

This vestige of Edwardian opulence has become a legend since its doors opened in 1907. Zelda Fitzgerald danced in the fountain out front, Solomon R. Guggenheim lived reclusively in a suite, surrounded by art, and the Beatles were guests on the occasion of their U.S. debut.

Flags flying from the Fifth Avenue façade represent countries of important foreign guests and dignitaries. Built of white glazed bricks and marble, the eighteen-story hotel, designed by Henry J. Hardenbergh, is capped by balustrade balconies and a massive cornice, rising to a green copper-and-slate mansard roof with dormers, gables, and minarets. The vistas, north to Central Park and east to Grand Army Plaza, make the hotel one of the most prestigious sites in the city. Visitors will notice hanging in the hotel's south hall a curious portrait of a young girl: she is Eloise, the fictitious resident of the Plaza and heroine of Kay Thompson's children's books.

TIMES SQUARE

(42ND STREET AND BROADWAY)

TIMES SQUARE IS CONTINUALLY REINVENTING ITSELF. A ONETIME GOAT FARM, THE AREA BECAME POPULAR WHEN THEATERS BEGAN MOVING IN AT THE TURN OF THE CENTURY. THE SQUARE'S NAME WAS INSPIRED BY THE *NEW YORK TIMES* AFTER THE PAPER BUILT ITS OFFICE TOWER AT THE SOUTH END OF THE SQUARE IN 1904. THAT NEW YEAR'S EVE, AN ILLUMINATED BALL WAS LOWERED FROM THE FLAGPOLE OF THE TIMES TOWER AND A TRADITION, THAT HAS SINCE BECOME WORLD-FAMOUS, WAS BORN.

BY THE 1920S, MOVIE COMPANIES BEGAN ERECTING GRANDIOSE PALACES AND THE ENTIRE DISTRICT WAS ELECTRIFIED WITH SPECTACULAR SIGNS AND MARQUEES—NO WONDER IT WAS CALLED "THE GREAT WHITE WAY." BY THE LATE 1960S, SQUALOR, PORNOGRAPHIC SHOPS, AND CRIME TURNED TIMES SQUARE INTO A SORDID, DANGEROUS NEIGHBORHOOD. IN THE MID-1990S, GOVERNMENT AND CORPORATE SPONSORS BEGAN REVITALIZING THE NEIGHBORHOOD: MORE THE-ATERS WERE RESTORED; RESTAURANTS, STORES, AND OFFICE BUILDINGS WERE BUILT; AND TIMES SQUARE RECLAIMED ITS PREVIOUS GLAMOUR.

Performances, assortments, resumes / Up Times Square to Columbus Circle lights / Channel the congresses, nightly sessions, / Refractions of the thousand theatres, faces / Mysterious kitchens. . . . You shall search them all /

—Hart Crane

Broadway at night. Cellophane. The new-ness. The vitality . . . it's inspiring. Just bring your own contents. And you create a sparkle of highest power.   —Anaïs Nin

THEATER DISTRICT

(41st to 59th streets, Eighth

to Sixth avenues)

The name Broadway is synonymous with the theater, and the district boasts many historic theaters, the New Victory among them. Built by Oscar Hammerstein I, it is the theater district's oldest performance space. The New Amsterdam, directly across from the New Victory, was home to the Ziegfeld Follies and is one of the few buildings in the United States constructed and decorated entirely in the art nouveau style. After many years of neglect, this theater has been superbly restored by the Disney Corporation.

CENTRAL PARK
(59TH TO 110TH STREETS, FIFTH AVENUE TO CENTRAL PARK WEST)

The character (of the park) is a poetic one and it is to be produced by means of scenes, through observation of which the mind may be more or less lifted out of moods . . .

— *Frederick Law Olmsted*

COMPLETED IN 1873, IT TOOK NEARLY TWENTY YEARS TO BUILD THIS 840-ACRE MAN-MADE LANDSCAPE, WHICH IS LARGER THAN MONACO. MORE THAN FORTY MILLION TREES WERE PLANTED, HALF A MILLION CUBIC YARDS OF TOP-SOIL WERE BROUGHT IN, AND TEN MILLION CART-LOADS OF EARTH WERE REARRANGED TO CREATE THE ROLLING HILLS, TRICKLING STREAMS, AND WINDING PATHS. FREDERICK LAW OLMSTED, WHO DESIGNED THE PARK WITH CALVERT VAUX, ENVI-SIONED THE PARK AS A LESSON IN DEMOCRACY, A PLACE WHERE PEOPLE FROM ALL WALKS OF LIFE COULD COME TOGETHER AND ENJOY A GREAT RUSTIC PARADISE.

CENTRAL PARK   63

The city seen from the Queensboro Bridge is always the city seen for the first time, in its first wild promise of all the mystery and beauty in the world. — F. Scott Fitzgerald

Among the wealthiest neighborhoods in the world, the Upper East Side is full of contrasts and contradictions—an interesting mix of skyscrapers, bistros, and beautiful old mansions. Many of the grand old houses, such as the Gertrude Rhinelander residence (Madison and 72nd Street) have been converted into elegant shops, art galleries, and houses of haute couture. Children can find recreation at Central Park's model-boat pond, while art lovers can enjoy "Museum Mile," the profusion of cultural institutions along fifth avenue from 70th to 104th streets.

It is a palace of art ... that sits there at the edge of the Park roaring with a radiance.

—Henry James

THE METROPOLITAN MUSEUM OF ART

(FIFTH AVENUE AND 82ND STREET)

THE METROPOLITAN MUSEUM OF ART WAS FOUNDED IN 1870, WHEN A GROUP OF CIVIC-MINDED NEW YORKERS DECIDED THAT THE CITY SHOULD HAVE AN ART MUSEUM IN THE EUROPEAN STYLE. THERE WERE NO FUNDS AND NO ART, BUT IN A LITTLE MORE THAN A CENTURY THE METROPOLITAN BECAME ONE OF THE FINEST MUSEUMS IN THE WORLD. THE ORIGINAL GOTHIC STRUCTURE WAS BUILT IN 1880 (CALVERT VAUX & J. WREY MOULD). OVER THE YEARS MANY NOTABLE ARCHITECTS HAVE BEEN INSTRUMENTAL IN ITS EXPANSION, INCLUDING: RICHARD MORRIS HUNT, DESIGNER OF THE FRONT FAÇADE; McKIM, MEAD, & WHITE, DESIGNERS OF THE NORTH AND SOUTH WINGS; AND ROCHE, DINKELOO, & ASSOCIATES, DESIGNERS OF THE GLASS WALL ADDITIONS. IT HOUSES AN ENCYCLOPEDIC COLLECTION OF MASTERPIECES OF WORLD CULTURES.

WHITNEY MUSEUM OF AMERICAN ART

(Madison Avenue at 75th Street)

This unusual granite-clad Bauhaus-style building, with its base narrower than its upper stories, was designed by Marcel Breuer in 1966. Specializing in twentieth-century American art, the museum evolved from Gertrude Vanderbilt Whitney's private collection. In 1931 she opened the museum in Greenwich Village as a showcase for emerging American artists—a mission that continues today with the Whitney's controversial biennial exhibitions.

Let each man exercise the art he knows.

—Frank Lloyd Wright

SOLOMON R. GUGGENHEIM MUSEUM

(Fifth Avenue and 89th Street)

In 1927, Solomon R. Guggenheim, a silver and copper mine magnate, saw modernist painter Baroness Hilda Rebay Von Ehrenwiesen about a portrait commission. The baroness, who believed that abstract art had mystical qualities, introduced Guggenheim to Klee, Kandinsky, and Frank Lloyd Wright—the rest is history. Completed in 1959, the museum that Wright designed to house the Guggenheim Collection is as singularly sculptural as the art itself. Its "organic" spiral form is in contrast to the traditional neighboring Fifth Avenue buildings. The impressive collection includes works by Picasso, Chagall, Calder, and Mondrian.

New York is a stone garden. Stone plants send up stems of varying height . . . a jungle where cathedrals and Greek temples balance on stilts. —Jean Cocteau

COLUMBUS CIRCLE MARKS THE ENTRANCE TO THE UPPER WEST SIDE. THE STATUE OF COLUMBUS (CREATED BY ITALIAN-AMERICAN SCULPTOR GAETANO RUSSO) HAS AN EXACT MATE IN MADRID, SPAIN (SINCE SPAIN SUPPORTED COLUMBUS ON HIS JOURNEY); THE TWO STATUES FACE EACH OTHER ACROSS THE ATLANTIC.

THE UPPER WEST SIDE IS KNOWN FOR ITS OPULENT APARTMENT BUILDINGS AND COZY TOWNHOUSES. IT IS ALSO A WELL-ESTABLISHED HAVEN FOR WRITERS, INTELLECTUALS, AND PERFORMING ARTISTS.

LINCOLN CENTER FOR THE PERFORMING ARTS

(62nd to 66th streets, Columbus to Amsterdam avenues)

Lincoln Center comes to life at night, when the fountain is lit, the chandeliers sparkle, and people sit at the outdoor cafe. The sleek 1960s-style buildings are made of travertine.

The Metropolitan Opera House (Wallace K. Harrison, 1966), the central structure of the plaza, is the most dramatic, with its gold-leaf ceiling, Austrian crystal chandelier, and pair of gold-leaf Chagall murals—all of which are visible from the plaza.

The New York State Theater is the most elegant, with its grand foyer and second-story loggia running the length of the façade. It is the home of the New York City Opera as well as the New York City Ballet. Other buildings in the complex include Avery Fisher Hall (home to the New York Philharmonic), the Library of the Performing Arts, and the Juilliard School of Music.

ANSONIA HOTEL

(BROADWAY BETWEEN 73RD AND 74TH STREETS)

THE ANSONIA IS ONE OF NEW YORK'S LEGENDARY APARTMENT BUILDINGS. WHEN THIS BEAUX ARTS EXTRAVAGANZA WAS CONSTRUCTED AS A HOTEL (GRAVES & DUBOY, 1904), LIVE SEALS PLAYED IN THE LOBBY FOUNTAIN, APARTMENTS WERE EQUIPPED WITH FAUCETS THAT RAN ICE WATER, AND CHICKENS AND GOATS LIVED ON THE BUILDING'S ROOF TO ENSURE FRESH PRODUCE. SOME OF THE FAMOUS ANSONIA TENANTS INCLUDED CARUSO, ZIEGFELD, STRAVINSKY, TOSCANINI, JACK DEMPSEY, AND BABE RUTH.

DAKOTA APARTMENTS

(72ND STREET AND CENTRAL PARK WEST)

BUILT IN 1884 (HENRY J. HARDENBERGH), THE DAKOTA WAS NEW YORK'S FIRST LUXURY APARTMENT HOUSE. A LIST OF ITS PAST AND PRESENT TENANTS INCLUDE LAUREN BACALL, LEONARD BERNSTEIN, JUDY GARLAND, AND JOHN LENNON. "STRAWBERRY FIELDS" IS LOCATED DIRECTLY ACROSS THE STREET IN CENTRAL PARK; THIS MEMORIAL LANDSCAPED TERRACE FOR THE DECEASED BEATLE CONTAINS A CIRCULAR MOSAIC OF ITALIAN MARBLE SPELLING OUT THE WORD "IMAGINE."

SAINT JOHN
THE DIVINE

(112TH STREET AND AMSTERDAM AVENUE)

ALTHOUGH IT IS ONLY TWO-THIRDS COMPLETE, SAINT JOHN THE DIVINE IS ALREADY THE LARGEST GOTHIC CATHEDRAL IN THE WORLD. BOTH NOTRE DAME AND CHARTRES COULD FIT INSIDE THE STRUCTURE WITH ROOM TO SPARE. THE WORK ON THE EPISCOPALIAN CATHEDRAL WAS STARTED ON DECEMBER 27, 1892, BY HEINS & LA FARGE, WHO DESIGNED IT IN THE BYZANTINE-ROMANESQUE STYLE. AFTER THEIR DEATHS THE WORK WAS TAKEN OVER BY RALPH ADAMS CRAM (OF CRAM & FERGUSON), WHO REDESIGNED IT IN THE GOTHIC-REVIVAL STYLE. CRAM & FERGUSON CONTINUED BUILDING IN THE FRENCH-GOTHIC STYLE UNTIL WORK WAS HALTED BY WORLD WAR II. TODAY THE CONSTRUCTION CONTINUES, USING METHODS AND ELEMENTS THAT DATE BACK TO MEDIEVAL TIMES. COMPLETION IS SCHEDULED FOR THE YEAR 2050.

We drove around Harlem for awhile awestruck by the whole scene. . . . It was beautiful, just beautiful. People in the streets, and nightclubs all over, nightclubs whose names were legendary.

—Cab Calloway

HARLEM AROSE IN THE 1880S WHEN BUILDING SPECULATORS, ANTICIPATING THE NEW SUBWAY, BUILT HUNDREDS OF APARTMENTS. WHEN HARLEM FAILED TO ATTRACT A WHITE MIDDLE CLASS, A BLACK AGENT NAMED PHILIP A. PAYTON WAS CALLED IN TO ATTRACT BLACKS TO THE NEW DISTRICT. BY THE 1920S, HARLEM BECAME THE SPIRITUAL HOME OF BLACK AMERICA, AND THE ACTUAL HOME TO LANGSTON HUGHES, COUNT BASIE, AND DUKE ELLINGTON. THE JAZZ TRADITION CON-TINUES TODAY AT THE APOLLO THEATER, WHERE BESSIE SMITH AND BILLIE HOLIDAY ONCE ENTER-TAINED, WITH LIVE SHOWS AND SPIRITED AMATEUR NIGHTS. THE LENOX LOUNGE, WITH ITS ART DECO FAÇADE AND CLASSIC SEMI-CIRCULAR BAN-QUETTES, REFLECTS HARLEM'S HEYDAY.

*The islands in the river and the glitter upon the twilight bridge . . .
once away, you do not remember, all that is left is the ghostly echo of
haunting wonder.* —Truman Capote

Quotation Sources

1. JACQUELINE KENNEDY ONASSIS: Powell, Kenneth. Grand Central Terminal: Warren and Wetmore (London: Phaidon Press Ltd., 1996), p. 24.

6. TONI MORRISON: Morrison, Toni. Jazz. (New York: Alfred A. Knopf, 1992).

8. GRACE PALEY: Quoted in "The Style of New York," New York Magazine, December 24-31, 1984.

10. JOHN DOS PASSOS: Quoted in New York U.S.A. Knopf Guides (New York: Alfred A. Knopf 1994), p. 177.

12. WALT WHITMAN: Whitman, Walt. "Crossing Brooklyn Ferry" in Mark Van Doren, ed., The Portable Walt Whitman (New York: Penguin, 1973), page 154.

20. E.B. WHITE: The Essays of E. B. White (New York: Harper Collins, 1992), p. 124.

35. EDITH WHARTON: "A Little Girl's New York" in Frederick Wegener, ed. The Uncollected Critical Writings of Edith Wharton. (Princeton, NJ: Princeton University Press, 1996), p. 274.

40. ARTHUR MILLER: Quoted in Jean Nathan, "Within the Walls of the Chelsea," The New York Times, February 9, 1993.

42. H.G. WELLS: Still, Bayrd. Mirror for Gotham: New York as Seen by Contemporaries from Dutch Days to the Present (New York: Fordham University Press, 1994), p. 280.

44. WOODY ALLEN: Cole, William, ed. Quotable New York: A Literary Companion (New York: Penguin Books, 1992), p. 15.

46. HENRY JAMES: The Portable Henry James (New York: The Viking Press, 1975), pp. 536-537.

53. ROBERT A.M. STERN: Quoted in "The Style of New York," New York Magazine, December 24-31, 1984.

58. HART CRANE: The Bridge (New York: Liveright, 1992), p. 65.

60. ANAIS NIN: The Early Diary of Anais Nin: Vol. II 1920-1923 (New York: Harcourt, Brace, Jovanovich, Inc., 1982).

63. FREDERICK LAW OLMSTED: Barlow, Elizabeth. Frederick Law Olmsted's New York (New York: William Alex Praeger Publishers in association with the Whitney Museum of American Art, 1972), p. 63.

64. F. SCOTT FITZGERALD: Fitzgerald, F. Scott. The Great Gatsby (New York: Charles Scribner's Sons, 1925) p. 63.

66. HENRY JAMES: The Portable Henry James.

68. FRANK LLOYD WRIGHT: Ziga, Charles J. New York Landmarks: A Collection of Architecture and Historic Details (New York: Dovetail Books, 1993), p. 58.

71. JEAN COCTEAU: Phelps, Robert, ed. Jean Cocteau: Professional Secrets (New York: Farrar, Straus & Giroux, 1970), p. 179.

74. JACK FINNEY: Finney, Jack. Time and Again (New York: Random House, 1970), pp. 57-60.

78. CAB CALLOWAY: Excerpt from Cab Calloway and Bryant Rollins "Minnie the Moocher and Me," in Robert Gottlieb, ed. Reading Jazz: A Gathering of Autobiography, Reportage, and Criticism from 1919 to Now (New York: Pantheon, 1996), p.117.

80. TRUMAN CAPOTE: Schwartz, Alan V., ed. A Capote Reader (New York: Random House, 1987) p. 296.